Book Two

BEDTIME STORIES OF THE SAINTS

Frank Lee, C.SS.R.

LIGUORI
PUBLICATIONS

One Liguori Drive
Liguori, Missouri 63057
(314) 464-2500

Imprimi Potest:
Edmund T. Langton, C.SS.R
Provincial, St. Louis Province
Redemptorist Fathers

Imprimatur:
+ John N. Wurm, S.T.D., Ph.D.
Vicar General, Archdiocese of St. Louis

Cover Design and Illustrations: Jim Corbett

TABLE OF CONTENTS

1

MARY, MOTHER OF JESUS
The Mother of Us All

The fountain still bubbles in the marketplace of Nazareth. It is called "Mary's Fountain," and it has been there during all these 2,000 years and longer. This is where the Mother of Jesus was born. Someday you may get the chance to visit there. If so, you will lift your eyes to the surrounding hills, and you will quickly come to love this country. Simply glorious views await you at every side: rich pastures, vineyards strong with fruit, pleasant gardens, charming valleys, and majestic mountains marching away into the horizon.

As you walk along you will come to the village well. These are the streets and bypasses and shortcuts that Mary knew. Like all the Hebrew ladies, she would usually be carrying a water jar on her shoulder as she went to draw water each morning.

Imagine what it would be like to turn a corner and run into Mary. Picture a woman meeting her and the young Jesus at her side. She keeps looking from the Child's face to the Mother's. "Dear heavens," she thinks, "they are exactly the same." Why not? He was all hers!

What did Mary really look like, this beautiful Mother of our Savior and of us all? Of course, there were no cameras in those days and no kind of portrait handed down by those who lived in her time. Some writers like simply to apply to her the Old Testament words from the "Song of Songs." Here is one of the lines: "You are all-beautiful, my beloved, and there is no spot in you." These are lovely words put on the lips of God when he speaks of us, his beloved. And, down through the ages, the Church has used them to describe how Mary must have looked.

But let us turn aside from our guesses about the appearance of Mary and turn to the New Testament to see what really happened in her life. We have to admit right away that the Bible speaks of Mary very seldom. Certainly, we do not have many words from her. But we do have incidents from her life.

Two Pictures of Mary

The first picture of Mary from the Bible sets the tone of her life. An angel of God has appeared to her and tells her that she has found great favor and grace with God, and that the heavenly Father asks her to bear an earthly Child who would save the world. Mary's answer was the story of her life, "Be it done to me according to your word."

The next picture of Mary is one that we often pass over all too quickly. Her cousin Elizabeth is to have a baby, and Mary makes that very long, special visit that delights her cousin. Elizabeth's own baby would be called John, and would prepare the way for Jesus' coming. The very first moment when Mary reached Elizabeth's home produced some of the loveliest words and thoughts of the whole Christian world.

The first part of our prayer called the "Hail Mary" is given to us by the angel: "Hail, Mary, full of grace. The Lord is with thee." Then Elizabeth adds her own inspiration: "Blessed art thou among women and blessed is the fruit of thy womb."

And now it is Mary's turn to sing to her Creator. The song is called the *Magnificat,* a word in which her heart cries to her soul to praise this great God:

"My whole heart and all of me shouts out that God is great. I am so filled with joy. I am so small, and yet he has singled me out from all people and they will call me the Blessed Mother. He is so great and powerful. And he has chosen me; the all-holy One has favored me. Now I have some little idea of how merciful he is to those who need mercy. Fear makes less sense when I know that God is talking about a mercy that explains fear.

"He is my great God. He fears no one and his mighty arm is my arm. He mixes up proud people who try to mix up me. This is the God of the poor and the hungry. He directs the rich to the sides of the road so I can walk by. There is food and drink and a roof for me. In his mercy, the great God has promised life and love to all the People of God, which means life and love for me, too, his chosen one."

Mary's Joy and Mary's Sorrow

A few months later, Mary gives birth to Jesus at Bethlehem. So, let's welcome Mary's Child.

Instead of saying a lot of pretty words, here is a question for you. Did you ever see that cartoon-movie around Christmas-time called the "Little Drummer Boy"? It tells how a young boy finally gets to stand before the tiny Jesus and do the only thing he knows how to do — make his drum talk for him. So there the little military fellow stands, his face all lighted with joy, as he beats out that glorious welcome to his little Lord Jesus. The angels welcome Jesus with a beautiful song; the drummer boy serenades him with the rhythm of his drum. We join the angels and the drummer boy every Christmas when we sing and do our thing for the baby Jesus, Mary's Son.

Mary was filled with joy at the birth of her Son. But soon after, she was faced with great sorrow. Obedient to the Jewish law, she and Joseph brought Jesus to present him in the Temple. Now there was a good, pious old man named Simeon who lived in Jerusalem at this time. The Holy Spirit was upon him, and he had been told that he would not die until he had seen the

Anointed of the Lord, as the Messiah was called. He came to the Temple this day, led by the Holy Spirit; and when the parents brought in the child Jesus and offered a pair of turtledoves to God in sacrifice and thanksgiving, Simeon took the Infant into his arms and blessed God in these words: "Now, Father, you can bring me home to heaven. You have fulfilled all your promises, and my eyes have seen this great light to all the peoples."

When the offering and presentation of Jesus were over, Simeon, shaking his head sadly, took Mary aside. He looked deeply into her eyes. "Mary, your Child — when he becomes a man — will be resisted by his people. Some will reject him, but

many will follow him; and, as for you, Mary, swords of sorrow shall pierce your heart."

Mary was so very young to be told this, and yet it had to be, because she was the one chosen by God to be the Mother of Sorrows and the Mother of Perpetual Help to the millions of us who would venerate her and love her and run to her when swords pierced our own hearts.

Mary's Son Grows Up

When Jesus was twelve years old it was time for him to be offered to God as a young Hebrew man. Of course, this is the rather sad hour when Jesus was lost in the Temple. The Bible tells us that Joseph thought Jesus was with Mary, and that Mary thought Jesus was with Joseph or with the returning townspeople of Nazareth, so they did not miss him for some time. But now days had passed and the awful truth had to be faced. Jesus was lost.

You know the rest of the story. It sort of turned out that Mary and Joseph were the ones who were lost. They did finally catch up with the Child-God after a three-day search, and Mary would never forget the sight of this one, her young Boy, explaining to the teachers of the law the meaning of the Bible. Forgetting about the dignity of the law, she ran to him and told him how worried they had been because they thought they had lost him. And that was the hour in which Mary was given a little clearer picture of her future. The young Christ spoke with seemingly cold words, "Did you not know I had to be in my Father's house?" The man of sorrows, the Redeemer, is talking here. He has his eyes on the Cross, and Mary, too, is taking its measurements.

Saint Luke brings to an end this scene of Mary's young motherhood and puts it this way: "Mary kept these things in her memory," or as we used to say so beautifully, "Mary treasured all these things and pondered on them in her heart." Anyway, they all went back to Nazareth, making sure this time to keep an eye on the young Man who happened to be a specialist in the Bible, *his* Bible.

Mary at the Wedding Feast

However, let us not be getting any idea of a scared, uninformed mother here. We shall soon see that we are dealing with a quite fine lady whom the Almighty has chosen to raise his own Child through childhood.

Remember the wedding in Cana of Galilee? Evidently, this young couple were Mary's friends and, obviously, they had run out of wine, which in those days was a very unhappy situation for the groom. Mary hears this terrible secret being passed around, and she turns to look at this Son of hers. There was a challenge and a smile in her eyes. "They have no more wine," she whispered. Really, it was a rather delightful moment. The Son looks at his Mother and says, "Woman, what does this have to do with you and me?" But it seems that Mary just kept looking at him; and if Jesus could get fidgety, he did. In fact, he said a very strange thing: "My hour has not yet come." (Up till then, he had never, as far as we know, worked a miracle. But because of what happened here, later on boys and girls with whom he had grown up in Nazareth would ask one another, "Isn't this the carpenter's Son?"

Anyway, Jesus and Mary exchanged that look again, and she told the servants, "Do whatever he tells you." We all know the rest. Jesus had the attendants bring large jars of water. He changed the water into wine and then directed the servants to take the liquid to the chief-taster. This was done, and that worthy man, the wine taster, cried out that they had saved the best till last, which was not the way it was supposed to be done. (But neither was the miracle!)

That is such a beautiful story that we are tempted just to sit there when the wedding crowd has gone and let the echo of Mary's words come back, "Do whatever he tells you." If only we would! If only we would *do whatever he tells us.* As we grow older we will find that this is not always so easy to do. But we have all heard of good, holy people who have been deeply hurt by someone's loss of health or property or wandering child, and they seem to be able to accept their problem by saying, "God's will be done." Mary can help us understand this.

Mary Follows Jesus

Now, after our Lord had left home and gone out to begin his preaching of the Good News about heaven being open to us, we are not going to be hearing very much about the Blessed Mother in the Scriptures. She knew that her Child had work to do for the Father. Now and then, however, as is only likely, she would follow him with her friends, and thus we come to this special day in their lives. Mary and these lady companions had joined the edge of a crowd of people who were listening to our Lord. A friend of the family had gone up to Jesus and quietly told him that his Mother was in the crowd. The next minute must have been quite a shock to Mary, even though Simeon had warned her that being the Mother of Jesus would not be easy. Anyway, Jesus chose not to return the whisper. Instead he picked that moment to cry out the way to reach heaven, "My mother? I'll tell you who my mother is — the one who does the will of my Father! That is my mother and my brother and my sister."

He is telling us that the one who accepts and lives by his Father's way and his Father's will and his Father's commandments is the one who is his mother and father and all. Of course, Jesus is not saying that Mary did not do the Father's will. He is saying, really, that all his children, including Mary and you and me, will reach heaven through accepting God's will. Especially Mary, for heaven's sake! She had based her whole life upon those words she spoke to the angel, "Be it done to me according to your word." That means according to God's holy will.

When we are young it is hard for us to understand how Jesus could treat his Mother this way. But we must put these words in the back of our hearts and take them out on the day that Jesus asks of us the price of being faithful to him. Yes, the words of Simeon the prophet are being whispered again in the background — "Swords of sorrow shall pierce your heart." It is the wedding feast of Cana all over again — "Do whatever he tells you." And here in this final scene with Mary before the Crucifixion, he tells the whole world, "If anyone wants to be my disciple, my follower, that person must deny himself or herself, take up the cross and follow me."

Mary at the Cross of Jesus

Mary can tell us what it means to take up a cross and follow him. She watched her Child reach for his Cross on that first Good Friday, and she would follow him very, very closely, right up front where no one else wanted to be, as he carried his Cross out to die for our sins. Yes, at last, she could freely follow in his footsteps, his blood upon her sandals.

She would stand there while they threw his body down upon the Cross. She would watch the hammers swing through the air again and again as her Child was nailed to the Cross. These were the hands she had kissed and fondled those many years ago. Then he was lifted up.

What a heart was the heart, and is the heart, of this great lady, Mary! She did not faint away. She stood beneath the Cross when every man's hand was turned against her Boy. She looked out from under the Cross, perhaps hoping to see his apostles, but there was only the one, John. The rest had run away.

Never forget that moment when our Lady watched her Son die so that you and I could be in heaven with him and her forever. No one wants this more than she does; and if the story of Mary will teach you to run to her, then it shall have done its work. After all, even Jesus had to run to her, as must any child run to his or her mother.

Now she was at the end of the road, and she had done it all so well.

To us it must mean that if she could be Mother of a God, then she could certainly be a mother to you and me. So our Lord cried out to all the world, "Behold, your mother!"

Now go to sleep.

2

SAINT ALPHONSUS LIGUORI
Missionary to the Poor

Part One

Do you know what it's really like to be poor? No doubt you have seen people who looked like they didn't know where their next meal was coming from. Your heart must have gone out to them, and you decided that when you grew up you would try to do something about it. Well, Alphonsus Liguori (leh-gó-ree), the saint we will talk about tonight, was like that. He looked around his world to find out why it was hurting and he went out to fix it. So this is the story of one man's war against poverty — of body and spirit; it is an invitation to join him where the action is as soon as you grow a little older.

Let's get our saint born and grown up: His trip through this world began on September 27, 1696. He had a fine mother. His father, related to kings, was a captain in the royal navy of Naples, and hard as nails. That was Don Joseph Liguori. He had planned Alphonsus' life and did not intend to put up with any back talk. Later on, he would be in for quite a surprise, but for the moment Alphonsus went right along the marked path. This first-born son, our saint, was father-planned for a life in the law courts, and so he obligingly won his diploma in civil law at the age of sixteen. Add to that a diploma in Church law, and we have a very young man all ready to become an expert in the whole field of law.

He did quickly become a success. Along with all the law knowledge, he was gifted in every way and could bring out these talents in beautiful, forceful language. It looked like the world was his oyster; all he had to do was open it. Meanwhile, back at the villa, his father was still running Alphonsus' life; he decided it was time for his son to marry. He gave Alphonsus a choice between two fair damsels. They were nice young ladies and Alphonsus was supposed to make up his mind and start hunting for an engagement ring and all that. Both ladies were of noble blood, and Don Joseph liked that part. But now the good Lord made his move. He, too, had quite a bit tied up in Alphonsus and his future. One of the young ladies suddenly broke and ran when she discovered that she was being treated like any piece of furniture while her father and Don Joseph did the bidding. Theresa, the lady in question, knew her rights and quietly let her father know that she had decided to spend and give her life to our Lord in the convent.

The other girl, Francesca, seems to have been quite willing to marry Alphonsus and was very pleasant to him at many parties. Our hero, on the other hand, kept looking around her, over her, and through her without ever noticing her. She decided that he needed a seeing-eye dog, not a wife.

Early Disappointment

Thus it was with Alphonsus in his young manhood. He was educated and had fine health. Now what?

Now this. There was a half million dollar property battle between a rich nobleman of Naples and a landowner of the kingdom of Tuscany. Alphonsus accepted the case for his fellow Neapolitan townsman. Bear in mind that thus far he had never lost a case before the courts. As ever, he was again very careful, studying seemingly every detail for a full month. Came the big day and everybody in Naples who was anybody headed for the courthouse. They got quite a dose. Oh, Alphonsus was great, argued beautifully, summed up masterfully, and sat down gracefully. Then the roof fell in. The other lawyer calmly presented Alphonsus and the court with a paper that our man had failed, or forgotten, to read. It spelled doom for the Neapolitan's case and for Alphonsus. (By the way, a "Neapolitan" is a native of Naples; and Neapolitan ice cream is something else again.)

People were filing out of court and whispering; they had doubts about the honesty of a certain Alphonsus Liguori. It was a bad day for him. However, Alphonsus was not too disheartened. He would just call for a fresh deck of cards and take another long look at this short game called "One Lifetime." This setback made him realize that the world with its "success" music theme had made him deaf to what life is all about. He spelled out, very loudly, right in court, how he felt: "This world will not fool me again! Good-bye, law courts and all that goes with you!"

It is an old truth that a great disappointment like that can either send us back to our little corner of pride to cry out the rest of our lives or it can make a man or a woman out of us, a knowing, tried, understanding person whom God can trust from now on. At this point of his life, we might say that Alphonsus was like the man our Lord found sitting near the pool of Bethsaida (beth-say´-dah). The water at times had miraculous powers to cure the sick person lowered into it. In the Gospel story, the ailing man told Jesus that he had no one to lower him into the water and that this had been going on for thirty-eight years. The Master looked him fully in the face and asked the big question: "Do you *want* to be healed?"

You see, that was the whole point. Was this man (or Alphonsus) really quite willing to stay comfortably sitting there in the shade of the porch of Bethsaida while others went out into a world of harsh cold and miserable heat, the marketplace of heroism and mistakes and loneliness? Alphonsus would answer that question with the rest of his life. He did *want* to be healed. His vocation and the vocations of all of us are very much tied up in our answer to that question. The light in our eyes and the blood in our veins have a calendar appointment with death. We can't waste all the beauty and power around us. We must get with it.

What Happened Afterward

Our saint left the courtroom, ran for his home, slammed his door, and stayed within for three days and nights. Meanwhile, Don Joseph, who had been out of town and missed the case, was trumpeting like a wounded elephant. As far as he was concerned, Alphonsus could stay in his room and starve to death. Things were not all that simple for the young lawyer. He knew that his father wanted him back in the courts. Would his conscience allow him to disobey? His education had cost his father much money. On the other hand, would he be destroying that conscience by turning back to the things of the world — the praise, the treasure, the temptation?

During these miserable days and nights, he was spending long hours at the Hospital for Incurables, helping in the smaller tasks, bringing comfort to the sick. Perhaps it was this kindness and self-denial that sort of opened up a wide window in his soul and let the grace of God come pouring in. And one day as he walked down the hospital corridor a voice sounded in his ear, "Leave the world and give yourself to me!" Everything around him seemed to be lit up and rocking; he just did manage to continue with his duties. Then it all happened again as he dressed to depart from the hospital, "Leave the world and give yourself to me." This time Alphonsus was ready. The lawyer in him had been trying the case all day: "Lord Jesus, too long have I resisted your grace; do with me what you will."

All the doubts and misgivings were suddenly gone down the drain. Alphonsus came out of the hospital and headed for the church of Our Lady of Ransom. He knelt before her shrine. Everything was caught up in a mystic light. He understood very clearly that God was asking him for his lifetime, for his dedication as a priest of the Most High. His prayers took the form of a complete offering. He would later hand over his great privileges as eldest son. Now, in a final gesture of decision and giving, he unbuckled his sword, the sign of nobility, and laid it on Mary's altar. From that hour onward he would devote himself only and absolutely to God and souls.

Struggle Between
Father and Son

To us, perhaps, the history of Don Joseph's efforts to keep his son out of the priesthood will seem to be a deadly, angry, sinful thing. We simply do not realize the tugs and pulls of those days; we do not fully understand all that was involved in being the eldest male child and thus expected to carry on the family name and glory. So we will see Don Joseph hurrying from pillar to post, trying every trick in the book to hold back Alphonsus. Finally, the Don suggested to Bishop Cavalieri, his brother-in-law, that the bishop help change the young man's mind. The answer was shattering: "What? I gave up my rights as a first son so I could find my soul's salvation in the priesthood, and now you want me to talk your son out of the same thing? You want me to risk his soul *and mine*?"

Don Joseph tried again, this time approaching the Cardinal of Naples. It was a repeat performance of putting the old neck on the old block. The conversation between them somehow brought out the fact that Alphonsus had a degree in Church law as well as civil law. The cardinal thought that this was just wonderful and that the young man could skip the seminary law course and be ordained a priest all the sooner. He recommended that Alphonsus enter the seminary immediately. Don Joseph reluctantly consented. So, on October 2, 1723, Alphonsus was formally dressed in the cassock. However, the rose was almost lost among the thorns; Don Joseph would not even attend the affair. In fact, he would ignore his son for many and many a day.

Whose Vocation?

Perhaps we should clear the air about the idea of a vocation and what was the right and the wrong of the Liguori problem. Put it this way: Don Joseph Liguori, the father, had wanted to be a sailor and have a family. He chose that and he arrived at it. On the other hand, he sort of went blind when it came to his son enjoying the same right, the same freedom in choosing his way of life. Joseph wanted to decide two vocations, his own and his son's. Nothing doing! We each decide our own. For when our parents are gone we still have to live out our lives, and heaven help us if we chose our vocations to please our parents when our hearts and spirits were somewhere else all the time.

Look ahead through the years of your life. Imagine yourself on your deathbed. How shall you want to have lived out your life? Then prepare yourself to live it that way, so that when you come to the end you can say, "I lived it the way I wanted to. I have no regrets." Don't die groaning, "If only . . . If only I . . . ."

We don't mean that the human side has no pull. Saint Alphonsus discovered that only too well. It was bad enough to be ignored by his father, but gradually his old friends began to hint that he was a bit of a moon child, a lunatic. But Alphonsus took it all on the chin. He had made up his mind that his life belonged to our Lord in the priesthood, and nothing, but nothing, was going to get in the way and stay there.

For him it was time to put away the toys and be his own man. He took a long look at the rules for students living outside the seminary and followed them, no matter what. Each morning he would serve at Mass, and his Sunday was given over to assisting at devotions in the various churches. Gradually, Neapolitans became accustomed to this new sight — the seminarian Liguori gathering his children from the streets for their catechism lessons. The youngsters would always be his special group, especially the poor ones; he would call them his abandoned ones, and throughout his life they would always be his chief concern.

Now go to sleep. We'll finish this another time.

Part Two

(We are talking about St. Alphonsus Liguori, born in Naples, Italy, almost 300 years ago. He studied Church and civil law and became a practicing lawyer at the age of sixteen. His father wanted him to marry, but Alphonsus thought otherwise. After losing an important case in the law courts, he decided that he wanted to become a priest. We left him as he was about to complete his days in the seminary.)

Alphonsus Becomes a Priest

The years of studying fly fast for a seminarian. For Alphonsus they ended gloriously on the morning of December 21, 1726. The eldest son of Liguori was ordained a priest forever. He was thirty years old, and it is interesting to watch his chosen activities in those early years. He had a sort of built-in compass that always pointed to the most abandoned and neglected souls. Many dioceses have a connection with the foreign missions, and Alphonsus was quick to join the local branch, called the Neapolitan Propaganda. Not content with this, he went on to associate himself with a group of Neapolitan priests who dedicated themselves to the work of bringing spiritual aid to condemned prisoners. We do not mean in all this that Alphonsus drew a hard and fast line between the forgotten and the remembered; rather, he just felt drawn toward those for whom no one else cared or where the supply was short amongst those who did care.

On the other hand, the once-famous lawyer, who 200 years later would be known mostly for his writings, was suddenly the preacher of the day. He had listened to the preachers of the time and he could not stand them. There were a lot of fancy words and gestures, and the preacher seemed more interested in himself than in the people. Alphonsus went in another door — he used simple, clear, inspiring words that even the most unschooled could understand. His listeners came from every group of society; all people need the pure word of God preached to them. Very soon even the nobility and educated classes found themselves at Alphonsus' feet. He had a deep love for our Lord and it came right through to the people, rich and poor alike.

It was this very simplicity and sincerity of his preaching that brought about one of the dearest moments of his life. He was giving a talk at the Church of the Holy Spirit, and on this night had no idea of the unusual visitor who sat in a darker section of the church. Sure enough, it was Don Joseph, the man of a thousand silences. However, on this evening he turned out to be just one more fish for Alphonsus to catch on his sermon hook. The old man came running up afterward to embrace his boy and cried out: "My son, how grateful I am to you! You have taught me really to know God. I bless you and thank you a thousand times for entering a life so holy and pleasing to God."

By this time, Alphonsus was preaching what might be called a "perpetual mission," a set of serious talks about life and afterlife. He had been gathering loafers and beggars and anyone else who would listen in the city streets, but the civil authorities were getting nervous and Alphonsus was told that his crowds were blocking traffic. The wind that blessed was still blowing his way, however, and various groups came forward to offer him their halls and chapels.

It was a perfect setup for the many forgotten who, dressed in rags, did not want to show up in a church. These castoffs, as well as merchants, lawyers, writers, and even priests, formed a terrific group, calling themselves the Association of the Chapels. They would meet every evening, say the rosary, listen to Alphonsus preach, have a confession period, and then move out to visit the sick around town. The works of mercy really came to life, and once more Alphonsus was pointing directly toward his future work for souls and the founding of a group of men who would go to the front lines with Christ — where the action was.

Alphonsus left his father's house about three years after his ordination rather than become somewhat of a family house priest, as happened only too often in those days. With his father's blessing, he went to live in the Chinese college, a headquarters for missionaries working in the Far East. It was just what he wanted, a system of prayer and discipline and thought.

You, too, will come to a turning point in your life someday. Maybe you will have to face the same kind of problems that Alphonsus faced, even heartbreaks, in trying to find out where you belong in life. So, don't feel lonesome if the decision is difficult. Join the club. Just open your heart, pray, and talk to a priest or nun or Brother whom you like.

Alphonsus Founds the Redemptorist Congregation

Alphonsus had been asked to preach in the Scala cathedral. The town of Scala was some twenty miles from Naples. For Alphonsus, it was a town of destiny. There his life became deeply connected with two people, Monsignor Thomas Falcoia and Sister Celeste Crostarosa. Subconsciously, the camera of his mind moved in on the spiritually neglected children of the town, the spiritually abandoned shepherds outside town. That picture would never fade.

The facts began to be fed into the computer. Falcoia was the spiritual director of both Alphonsus and Sister Crostarosa. Through Falcoia's efforts, Alphonsus brought his fervor and legal mind to reorganizing Sister Crostarosa's convent rule. She, in turn, proved to be a woman of God and, after a series of visions, laid it on the line to Alphonsus that he was to found a society of priests and Brothers whose purpose and ideal was to use the parish mission to bring the forgotten back to God.

Alphonsus knocked on the doors of the brilliant and the holy in search of light and decision. The light they gave him was green. Go ahead. The decision found its moment of truth with his father, who once more appears as the "heavy" actor in the drama. He found Alphonsus at the Chinese college and their argument could be heard a block away:

Don Joseph: "I let you give up everything to be a priest, and now you want to throw it all away."

Alphonsus: "I became a priest because I wanted to throw everything away."

Don Joseph: "Let the country peasants teach their own children. I would rather have you breaking stones for the public roads."

This went on for three hours. The old man had stood still while his dreams of the family name and dignity went down the drain; he had watched all the years of legal training swept under the rug; and now, this — to be abandoned in his old age while his son became a wanderer on the uncharted mission roads. He physically clung to Alphonsus as though he would cement their very souls. One little word from the son could have shoveled all the misery out of that room. The word never came. Years later Alphonsus would say: "That was the strongest temptation I ever had in my life."

About that temptation: This is a master talking. Alphonsus meant it was that terrible, flat-out weakness that can almost floor a human being when slugged with one of those hard-core, dug-in, cliff-hanging "wantings." He really wanted to please his earthly father, but he wanted more to please his heavenly Father. So did Christ in the garden. "Father, take this chalice from me." And Christ answered himself with the only answer there is: "Not my will, but thine be done."

One man's decision — about 250 years ago. Shall we ask ourselves whether it was worthwhile? We would do better to ask the hundreds of thousands of country (and city) people who have found Christ or found him again beneath the banner of Liguori's men. Meanwhile, they are still out there, those Redemptorist priests and Brothers, from Alaska to Africa and on to any point of the compass you choose. Scratch a hut and you will find a Redemptorist priest just about any place in the world. Scratch it twice and you will discover the Redemptorist associate Brother holding up his end of the net, watching for the fish. As Scripture said about our Lord: "With him there is plentiful redemption."

Alphonsus wrote about 100 books after he was fifty years old, including an all-time best seller on devotion to Jesus' Mother. There is nothing light or simple about writing any kind of readable book, but this man took on a special challenge. Alphonsus wrote a moral theology, and that is like saying that a medical doctor takes time out to write the complete "how to" for all doctor's cases. Alphonsus was given the dynamite title that only some 30 human beings ever knew, "Doctor of the Church." That means that it is safe and sound to follow anything he has said about Church matters.

Alphonsus Becomes a Bishop

In 1762 a really unscheduled bomb dropped right in the middle of Alphonsus' busy life. He was made a bishop. Oh, he squirmed and yelled a bit, but Pope Clement XIII quietly ignored the noise and put him over the diocese of St. Agatha of the Goths. Our man drew a really long breath, took the bit in his teeth, and plowed up his diocese.

He began in his own house, where neither furniture nor food was better than that of the poorest family in his flock. With his deep conviction of the necessity of the parish mission, he made every pastor have one preached in his parish. Shrewdly, he had no Redemptorist missionaries on this work — there was to be no partiality; but missions there would be, even if he had to pay the expenses, as he often did.

The existing seminary was somewhat of a mess, due both to careless professors and the general bleakness of the buildings and surroundings. When Alphonsus had polished off that problem there were requests for admission from all over Italy.

Many of his nuns' convents were somewhat lavish boardinghouses for wealthy ladies who did not care to marry. They were scandalizing the population. Alphonsus brought in the female counterpart of his Congregation — the Redemptoristines. Their life of prayer and sacrifice was targeted at the fancy convents. The message got through. He was always a pushover for the poor, especially the spiritually poor, and the lavish convents were just that.

His effectiveness as a bishop might be best shown against the background of his efforts to resign. The pointed answers of the pontiffs run to a hard comedy. He tried first under Pope Clement XIII, advancing his illness and age as legitimate reasons. The answer came back: "His shadow alone is enough to govern the diocese."

He really was sick, so he tried again during the reign of Pope Clement XIV. The answer came back: "It is enough for me if he governs his diocese from his bed."

Pius VI was the next pope. He, too, at first refused to accept the resignation. But Alphonsus was 83 years old, almost blind, almost deaf. The pope finally let him go.

The Death of Alphonsus

We wish there could be a happy ending, humanly speaking, to all this. But there was no happy ending. Alphonsus died outside his own Congregation of priests and Brothers. For our purpose here we will simply say that there were two groups of Redemptorists, one centering around Rome, the other around Naples. The blind Alphonsus signed a paper whereby he unknowingly accepted a rule that placed all authority in the hands of the King of Naples. It was a sham Redemptorist rule that outraged everything Alphonsus had lived for, fought for, and would die for. For this an enraged Rome cut him off.

So he died that way, this man with the impossible dream — impossible in the courts of man, but run-of-the-mill in the courts of God.

Later, of course, all these matters were straightened out. The very pope who had caused our saint so much suffering repented this way: "I have been persecuting a saint." And Alphonsus was declared just that by the Church in 1839. If ever life seems meaningless to you, remember this man who met its challenge head-on and lived it to the hilt.

Now go to sleep.

3

SAINT NICHOLAS
The Original Santa Claus

Boys who go to the seminary (to become priests) and girls who enter the convent (to become nuns) warmly remember the days they spent there. Some days were utterly forgettable, while others were absolutely unforgettable. One such day in the life of a certain young seminarian was the feast of St. Nicholas. Speaking for his entire class, he describes it in the following way.

We will never forget our first St. Nicholas Day, December 6. Seminaries, of course, do not exactly load the students down with candy and cake; and so we were surprised when we went down to our big dining room on St. Nicholas Day. There we found all kinds of candy and cookies and cakes, more delicious than the kinds we had been dreaming of since we had left home and our mothers' stoves.

Maybe, we thought, the seminary superiors have had a change of heart and this is all part of a new and wonderful policy: candy and cake every night! Then the priest in charge of us sang out: "Happy St. Nicholas Day to everybody!"

Well, the mystery was solved, and we were grateful to St. Nicholas for the treat, but we hated to see that "new policy" dream sail out the window.

Later on that evening, Father told us about the great celebrations on St. Nicholas Day in Germany and Switzerland and Holland. Over there, people (especially children, for it is their special day) receive their gifts on St. Nicholas Day instead of on Christmas Day. The good Sisters who prepared all our meals had recently come from Bavaria. And they were giving us the same kind of treat they had received when they were little girls back in their homeland.

And why all this celebrating and giving of presents on St. Nicholas' feast day? Well, that is the story we will tell tonight.

But, before we begin, we must make something clear about these thousand-year-old saints like Nicholas. Sometimes we can tell you only what has been handed down to us by way of parent to child and so on through the centuries. In other words, nobody knew how to print a book until hundreds of years after an early saint like Nicholas lived and died. So there were no magazines or newspapers or anything that could have printed all the news about St. Nicholas, and then be put away safely so we could read it hundreds of years later.

And besides all that, these great people were dying by the thousands for our Lord; they were all saints and martyrs for him, and only God knew which one would be especially put aside to be given a place of honor on our altars for all the centuries to come. So what we have are some "handed down" stories about our saint — "handed down," but as accurate as we can make them.

Good Saint Nick

Of course, we know when Nicholas lived. It was about three hundred years after our Lord died, and his town was a few hundred miles north of Nazareth, where Jesus grew up. His parents were good, devout people who turned out a good, devout boy.

They were rather wealthy, and after their deaths Nicholas found himself with quite a lot of money. He was a young man now, and his eyes were turned to God. He wanted to give away the money to poor people.

Then one day there came to him the news that a very poor man in the city needed help badly. He had three young

daughters who were hoping soon to be married. However, in those days, the bride's father had to give the husband a gift of money or property at the wedding. Now, since the father had nothing to give the future husbands, it looked like he was going to send the three girls out on the streets to beg for marriage money, and maybe to get into all kinds of trouble.

And now enters good St. Nick. The oldest girl was just about to be sent out into the streets, when very late at night our saint came quietly down the sidewalk to their house and dropped a bag of gold coins through the open window. And off he went. The girl was saved; the father gave the money to the young man who wanted to marry her, and so the gift of St. Nicholas helped them begin a good, holy marriage.

Well, you can guess the rest. Yes, St. Nicholas kept his eyes open, and when he saw that the next two young daughters were beginning to keep company with their young men, he came back twice, secretly, and quietly dropped a bag of gold coins through an open window and fled off into the darkness. And so everyone was happy, but especially Nicholas, who just wanted to give and not stand around waiting to be thanked or get a present in return. (That is real "giving.")

Word Gets Around

No doubt, someone saw Nicholas at his kind work, because before long the story was all over town. And as the years went by, that story took hold on thousands of people's minds, and they began to give their children gifts on St. Nicholas Day, just as he had given to those young girls. In many, many towns, a man would dress up like St. Nicholas (in a bishop's red robes; looking solemn in a big beard, with a staff in hand) and go from house to house on the eve of St. Nicholas, and find out how each child had been during that year.

After he had gone, the children would hang up their stockings and hope for the best. And then the next morning (if they had been good) they would find their stockings full of gifts and candy; but if they had been bad, they would find an empty stocking or, worse still, a switch in their stocking, with which they were to be spanked!

More years went by, and gradually two things happened which have a lot to do with our story. For one thing, St. Nicholas began to be called Santa Claus (Santa for *saint,* and Claus for the last part of a European spelling of *Nicholas*). Of course, the second thing that happened was that in this country the giving of gifts was put off until Christmas Day, our Lord's birthday. (By the way, what are you giving him for his birthday this year?) However, in many places across the ocean, St. Nicholas' feast on December 6 is still the day for presents. (So you see, there is a Santa Claus, just like your mommy and daddy told you.)

We can all see now how St. Nicholas and Santa Claus and Christmas are all sort of tied up together with the idea of "giving," not "getting." In other words, it would not be the spirit of Christmas or of St. Nicholas if children hid their presents for others until they found out whether those others were giving them something in return.

Don't let yourself become too "yourselfish" at Christmas. It is really a time for gifts — not necessarily those that cost a lot of money but rather those that give your *love* and your *obedience.* That is what our Lord gave on the first Christmas. Out of *love* for us, he gave himself to be our present; and out of love for his Father, he would be *obedient,* even to his Cross. What a gift he gave, and it will last forever!

Nicholas in Danger

Naturally, there is a lot more to our saint than being mixed up with Christmas presents. He lived in the time of the persecutions under a man named Emperor Diocletian (die-o-klee-shun). It took an awful lot of bravery to be a Christian in those days. In fact, the word "martyrs" did not by itself mean people who died for Christ. It simply meant that they admitted they were Christians. But because everyone who admitted that was put to death, after awhile "martyr" meant going all the way for him — life itself!

Anyway, the emperor, who was not a Christian but a pagan, adoring gods made of marble, would send out his soldiers to hunt people down, throw them into prison, torture them, and finally put them to death. That is what the "persecutions" meant. Imagine, then, how they treated St. Nicholas when they found that he was not only a Christian but a bishop! (Yes, by this time, our saint had become the bishop of a place called Myra, in Asia Minor.) And now he was taken to prison, tortured, and left there in chains. He was about to be put to death, but just then there took place one of the greatest happenings in the Christian Church.

For some years there had been fierce battles between the three or four generals who wanted to be the next Roman emperor. A really great man, Constantine (con-stun-teen), finally won out. And this in a very strange way. He was about to fight General Maxentius (max-en-shus), who had a much larger army than he. Then, on the night before the battle began, Constantine had a vision of a great cross and underneath it were the words: "In this sign you will conquer." Constantine believed that the God of the Christians was on his side, and he had all his soldiers paint the name of Jesus on their shields. On the next day he met the enemy and destroyed them. It was a victorious moment for Christ on earth, and it would take the thousands of Christians out of their prisons, their caves, and their chains.

And, happily, out popped St. Nicholas too.

Nicholas Fights for Truth

There is one story about St. Nicholas that we sort of like, even though some say it is only a legend. There was a church council at Nice (like the worldwide Council that Pope John called in Rome some years ago). One of the men who came there was Arius, and he was preaching some very unhappy things about our Lord. He did a lot of harm. So St. Nicholas walked up and — well, he slugged him. Our saint was promptly put in jail, but our Lord quietly let him out.

Nicholas truly did hate evil. He hated the silly worship of a statue made of marble, hated paganism. He was great for knocking over the temples of false gods, the devils screaming at him as they left town.

One thing in all this is sure, that whatever he did, the people loved him, honored him, prayed to him as a saint after his death. The world is full of altars and churches dedicated to him. Even as far back as seven hundred years ago, there were four hundred churches dedicated to St. Nicholas in England alone. He is the patron saint of Russia, the special patron of Moscow. (May he knock some sense into their heads as he tried to do with Arius!)

Out of the dimming pages of his life comes one other great truth. He loved children. He was forever teaching them the importance of innocence and goodness; and he constantly reminded their parents that they could not, dare not, teach a child one thing and then themselves do the opposite.

So now you know the story of quite a wonderful patron and saint who is still praying for you. There is one other group for whom he is patron, but I doubt that you will have to approach him under that title, which is "patron of pawnbrokers." Yes, those three golden balls that used to hang outside the pawnbroker's store (and still do in some places) were there in memory of (and prayer to?) the St. Nicholas who gave the three bags of gold coins to the troubled young girls. However, you had better check this out with your father before you visit a pawnbroker and put in a formal request for a bag of gold.

Please, in your prayers tonight, do remember that other sad little crowd, the children of Russia. St. Nicholas is also their patron. Pray that some day they may all come to hear of the Christmas story and know its warmth and love and beauty and the adorable gift of a baby God.

Now go to sleep.

4

SAINT MARTIN DE PORRES
The Barber Who Became a Saint

Can you imagine a dog and a cat and a mouse eating out of the same bowl at the same time? Well, they did; and here is the story of the man who got them to do it.

These are the days and nights of St. Martin de Porres, (pour-rays), and we shall find that he was a great barber, a great sweeper, and a great saint who loved people and animals. His love for all of God's creatures is the story of his life.

St. Martin lived some 400 years ago. His mother was a beautiful black woman, and his father belonged to the family of the king of Portugal. Martin was born in Lima, the capital city of the South American country of Peru. His mother was very devout and taught her children to be children of God. And while we are speaking of his childhood we might run in here a little problem that may come your way. Martin had been taught to love the poor, but sometimes he overdid it. His mother would give him money to buy food for supper, and he would often give it all away. That was not so good because then his mother and sister had to go hungry. Kindness is not really kindness when we hurt someone else in the picture.

Martin Goes to School

Martin's father wanted him to become a barber. In those days, however, a barber did more than cut hair. He did most of the doctoring in the neighborhood. He would fix up broken legs, give out medicine, and cut hair, all in one sitting. In fact, that's why — even to this day — the barber's pole seen outside his shop looks like a huge peppermint stick. (The white and red pole represents clean bandages wrapped around a bleeding wound.) Martin studied to be this kind of barber — not to become famous, but because he loved people and wanted to take pain out of their lives.

So, Martin went to school to learn his trade, but there was a different kind of schooling that the boy's heart was really wanting. Deep down, day by day, the call came louder and louder. Martin wanted to go to the school of the love of God. He wanted to enter a monastery, a place where he could give himself completely to God and his plans. Nothing and nobody could stop him. On the Cross our Lord cried, "I thirst." So did Martin. He thirsted for the souls for whom Jesus had died, and he wanted to fill up the thirst of our Lord with the love of people like you and me. Martin knocked on the door of the Dominican Monastery of the Holy Rosary in Lima. He was about 16 years old.

With his father's great name, de Porres, Martin could have gone up very high in the Church. Instead, he deliberately became a *donado.* That is a Spanish word, and in English it would simply mean a donation, a gift. Martin would not become a priest or even a Brother who helps the priests in their work, but, instead, he would be a servant of priest and Brother. He would work in the fields, sweep the monastery, and just be a gift to God 24 hours a day. Martin would never turn back from his *donado,* his gift of himself. He was firm, not stubborn. (Mother, please explain the difference.) We all have a right to choose our way of life, and Martin stood by his choice. Someday he would be the greatest glory of the family de Porres.

Meanwhile, back at the monastery, he became a great sweeper. He did not like dirt, and he swept up everything that was not nailed down, so to say. No job was too grimy for him and his broom. And even to this day, the people of South America wear tiny brooms on his feast day.

But, in truth, the doctor side of our saint was called for more and more. Martin did not mind this at all. He knew that sickness could really be painful. When you hurt yourself — even a little finger — your body can hurt all over; and you don't feel much like praying, do you?

So Martin always hurried to help those who were hurting. Of course, human beings are kind of ornery sometimes, and they would yelp when our barber-doctor touched the sore spot. One time, when Martin was taking care of one of his Brothers, he must have pressed too hard where it hurt, and the Brother cried out: "Take it easy, you good-for-nothing!"

Martin said to himself, "This one *really* knows me and tells me off. I must take special care of him, so he will keep me in my place."

As you can see, we have a pretty humble *donado* on our hands. But that was nothing next to what happened later on. It seems that the monastery was running out of money and food and everything. The superior put together a few of the rare old treasures of the monastery and went out to sell them. Martin heard about it and ran down the street after the superior. He caught up with him; and, all out of breath, he told him that he, Martin, could be sold as a slave, and then the treasures could be kept. The superior looked at him and his eyes filled with tears. "Go home, my son," he said. "Brother Martin is not for sale."

Gaining and Growing

What was happening in the soul of Martin all these days? This for sure: His faith became very alive to him. Most people go into a church and barely notice the statues as they walk by.

Not so for Martin; to him these were the people of heaven, crying out to him: "Come on! If we made it, you can. Courage!" (How about that?)

He asked the Blessed Mother to teach him how to pray. He surely learned from the best, and pretty soon he was able to pray even as he worked all day and half the night. Lima was a beautiful city, but it was loaded with sin, so Martin offered up his work and prayer to make it as beautiful inside as it was on the outside. He kept his own inside beautiful by going to confession and receiving Communion. For him, confession bathed and clothed his soul, and Communion strengthened him to remain clean and pure. No wonder that people who knew him said that just looking at him made them want to do better.

What was his greatest gift to you and to all children? Obedience would be it. Obedience was not a lot of "don'ts" to him; instead it was a big beautiful "do." And "do" meant to give his whole life in obedience to our Lord, just as our Lord spent his whole life in obedience to his Father.

(You may have noticed that nothing has been said about Saint Martin being black. Well, there's been no reason to do so. There are just God and people. Nothing else counts.)

So let's get back to Martin's days on earth. We were talking about obedience, which, by the way, does not mean that everybody is trying to push us around. No, it means that God has some things he wants done on earth, and we agree to get them done for him while we are here, the way Martin did. Remember that the next time your mother wants you to go to the store or do the dishes.

The more Martin gave himself to God, the more God gave himself to Martin. There were times when God lit up his mind in wonderful ways. For instance, on more than one occasion, while Martin was sweeping the halls of the monastery, he came upon some students deep in a problem they had in class that day. Martin would politely listen, give them the right answer, and get back to his broom. The students would just look at him, amazed. They knew he had never studied such things.

Martin's whole life brought out another great truth, namely, that busy people always have time to help, while lazy people spend twice that time explaining why they can't help. Martin did not believe in those slippery answers, such as "Wait a minute" (meaning several hours from now) or "I'm busy now, come back tomorrow" (meaning never come back).

Friend of the Animals

Now it is time to tell you about Martin and his animals, especially about his treaty of peace with the mice. This is really something, and it really happened. In the monastery, Martin had charge of the clothing and sheets and all that. Every night, however, a big gang of mice would feast on the cloth, and our Martin knew that this could not go on. One night he waited up in the dark and finally caught one of the little fellows. Martin had quite a talk with him. He told the mouse that if he, the mouse, would keep his gang out of the clothes closets, then Martin would feed them every day at the other end of the garden. It seems that the mouse went back and talked it over with the other bad guys; and then, suddenly, mice came from out the woodwork, the floor, every place, and all headed for the garden. The story had a happy ending; the mice kept their part of the bargain and Martin kept his.

There was nothing really so strange about this. If God loves his lilies, why shouldn't Martin love God's mice? They are all his creatures. And we can see now why it was not so hard for Martin to talk the dog and the cat and the mouse into eating together. In fact, there was one time when one of his Brothers heard Martin tell a cat to come back to the monastery the next

morning for a checkup on his broken leg. The Brother could not believe his ears, and was Johnny-on-the-spot the next morning, waiting to see what would happen. Sure enough, the cat was sitting there outside the door, and behind the cat was a turkey with a broken wing. Word really got around in the animal underground. Of course, they all knew that Martin would not hurt them, but you youngsters must not forget that our saint was very special. No child should ever pet a dog without asking his parents. (Not the dog's parents, silly!)

If we check out all the stories about Martin and his friends, it seems that the mice were his favorites. In fact, there are hardly any pictures of St. Martin in all of South America that do not have a mouse somewhere in them.

Adviser of Men

Meanwhile, many people came to visit Martin. Among them were the king's representative, the governor, the mayor, and all down the line. They came to him for advice, and at one time it was said that Martin was the power behind the throne. With the wisdom of a true child of God, he helped to run the great city of Lima.

He managed to keep his great gifts to himself as a rule, but there was one time when he almost let the cat out of the bag. (Not a real cat!) He was talking over a certain sickness with some doctors, and these words came out: "Yes, I saw this case treated in France." The doctors looked at Martin. They all knew he had never been out of South America. At least, they thought they knew. Actually, God had, in his own way, let Martin look in on the sickness and the cure in a French hospital.

With all this, it should come as no surprise that Martin once leaned over a dead Brother and whispered in his ear, "Brother Thomas!" And one hour later Brother Thomas was eating breakfast. Oh, yes, we have quite a patron saint for barbers and for everybody else.

This is the way that Martin lived. And when it came time for him to die, he felt, like so many saints, that life was such a short time in which to serve God and people and bring his love to them. Please God, that some day you, too, will carry Martin's burning torch of faith and love.

Now go to sleep.

5

SAINT THERESE
Little Saint for Little People

People like things big these days. The bigger they are the better they are supposed to be. But this is not always true. Sometimes the little things, the little people, are the best. And this is certainly true of the saint we will talk about tonight. Her name is Therese. She is called "Little" Therese not because she was small in size but because she became great by doing little things well.

Therese lived in France, in a town called Lisieux. She did not live very long, for our Lord called her to heaven when she was only twenty-four years old. That happened in 1897. Her life, as we shall see, was quiet and hidden. Yet, the whole world knew that she was a saint just a few years after she died.

Now it usually takes years and years after the death of a holy person before the Church declares that he or she is really a saint. Our little Therese beat out everybody; she made it in only twenty-eight years.

Being declared a saint is a very special affair. The pope and the bishops and others actually ask God to let everyone see, by a big miracle, that he, God, really is behind this person who is going to be canonized. When the Church canonizes someone she announces officially that this person has lived a life of true sanctity. It is something like getting elected into the Hall of Fame in heaven. The Church asks God not for a tiny miracle but a mighty one, like curing cancer or restoring sight to the blind. Things like that.

Therese as a Little Girl

Let's see, then, how Therese became so "pleasing to God" during her life and after her death. She had once been told by someone to write down her own idea of holiness, and this is the way she put it: "I want to be the Infant Jesus' rubber ball and let him roll me and bounce me or leave me alone beneath the table and just forget me . . . whatever he wants. I just want to be there when he wants me again." Children often treat their toys this way, even their favorite ones. Well, that's how Therese felt about the Infant Jesus; she wanted to be a toy in his hands.

What was Therese like when she was a little girl? Well, she was kind of grabby, like most of us. For instance, one day her older sister Leonie offered her a choice between some dolls and other toys. Therese came up with a fine answer, fine for Therese. She said, "I'll take everything."

(Later on, she would give that same answer when God sent her sufferings: "I'll take everything," sickness, death, all.)

But back to her childhood. She tells us that she wanted to be teacher's pet at school. She noticed that other girls tried it and did pretty well, enjoying special favors from the teachers. Therese got nowhere when she tried to be a favorite. When she grew up and looked back at those days she said, "Oh, happy first failure! From how many later unhappinesses you saved me!" She learned that teacher's pets are not always happy and are seldom popular with their schoolmates.

Now despite these childhood faults she did have a warm love for the Infant Jesus. (That is why she became known in the religious life as Therese of the Child Jesus.) And it is no wonder that she loved the Infant. Have you ever stood and looked into the crib of your baby brother or sister or maybe a neighbor's baby? Aren't they tiny, especially when they try to put their hand around your finger? And with one of your own fingers

you can roll them over on their backs. Therese felt this same kind of melting love for the Infant Jesus.

Therese Wants to Become a Nun

Very early in her life Therese began to think about going to the convent. Her two sisters had already joined the Carmelites, and now Therese wanted to follow them. But she was only fourteen years old and no girl was allowed to enter the convent before the age of sixteen. Both her bishop and the Carmelite Sisters said, "No, you are much too young!"

But Therese was determined. It was a very big year in Rome, and a special jubilee celebration for Pope Leo XIII was going on. Therese was to go along to Rome with her family, and she secretly made her own little plans. The day came when she and her family would be introduced to the Holy Father. When Therese's time came to kneel before the Holy Father, she blurted out: "Your Holiness, in honor of your jubilee year, please allow me to enter the Carmelite Sisters at fifteen." The Holy Father looked down at her and put his hand on her head. He was deeply impressed, but he said, "Not yet." He said he would pray, and he told her she was to pray and to watch for God's will.

She had been refused. As she took her father's arm and walked away, she wanted to cry. Then she realized that this was the game she had promised to play with Jesus. It had been her idea to be the ball, and now she was getting just what she had prayed for. She had said that Jesus could bounce her around and throw her away and even puncture her to see what the ball was made of. She had made her promise, and she would keep it. Prayer was the means she used to keep her hopes alive.

We don't have space here to go into the story of those prayers and hopes, but finally her prayers were answered. Yes, sir, yes, ma'am, one fine day the bishop said it was OK; the Carmelites said it was OK; and she knew that God was saying OK, too. Her prayers and her patience and her faith in God had finally led her to the life she had wanted so desperately for so long.

Her Life in the Convent

Now that she was in the convent, she really tried hard to get close to Jesus, especially in her prayers. Once she was asked what prayer meant to her. She gave the oldest answer in the world: "Prayer is the lifting of the heart to God." She really believed in Jesus' words, "Without me you can do nothing." In temptation she would run to him, turning her back on the devil. She did not see any sense in standing there and looking him in the face. Instead, she ran to our Lord and told him she would do anything for him. Now that's the way to fight temptation!

She was human enough to let the human problems get her down. Her place in chapel was right in front of a little old nun who was forever jingling and jangling her rosary. Therese found it very hard to pay attention to her own prayers. She prayed about this and then she got the idea (the *grace,* let's say) to make a prayer using the jingling, jangling of the rosary for background music. So instead of being upset by the pinglings and the panglings, she turned them into her silent little song to God. The maddening music became the melodious prayer.

She was truly an artist in her ways of loving God. On one occasion she put it this way: "I am a very little soul, so I can offer only very little things to our Lord." She was wise enough to know that most people hardly ever get the chance to do really big things for our Lord, and they could waste their whole lives just waiting for that chance. Therese was smart. She was satisfied to welcome the little splinters of the cross, the tiny everyday sacrifices and unkindnesses that came her way. These were always there. (For you, too!)

Before her death the Little Flower would know a lot about pain and weakness, and she did not think herself strong enough to be a girl giant. She knew she needed God's help and guidance. So she kept on reading and reading the Bible, until one day she opened the Book of Proverbs and found just what she had wanted and needed so long: "Whoever is a little one, let him come to me."

She knew then that God wanted her as she was right now — *little.* This sweet, young spirit, called Therese, would not waste a moment arguing with giant intellects about the existence of heaven. She was confident about what her heaven would be like.

A Shower of Roses

One day she promised, "I will spend my heaven doing good on earth." And again, like a messenger of God's plans, she told the world, "After my death I will let fall a shower of roses." This shower of roses was to be a long, long list of miracles to help those she left behind her, whatever their needs might be — spiritual or physical.

One of the most simple of these miracles happened in a place called Pela in South Africa. The little Christian convent children were gathered around an altar of the Sacred Heart. They were excitedly planning the decorations for the statue of our Lord. They wanted them to be the most beautiful ever, and for that they wanted some real roses.

Now in the convent garden stood one lone rosebush, dried and withered. For six years it had not produced a single blossom. The children decided to ask the Little Flower to help them, because, as they said, "She and roses are good friends." They began a special novena, nine days of fervent prayer, and on the seventh day of the novena buds broke out on the sad little plant. They grew very fast and their petals unfolded in the most magnificent color, a shade that the sacristy Sisters had never seen before. They were very different from any roses that had ever blossomed on that bush. This is a simple, lovely story — much like the Little Flower herself.

As we close our story of Sister Therese of the Child Jesus, let us think about what she is telling us. She is saying that she is little and that her way to heaven had to be little because she could not have made it any other way. To use her own words: "I cannot make myself greater; I must bear with myself just as I am with all my mistakes. I do want to seek a way to heaven, a new way, very short, very straight, a little path." Therese found that little way that the Infant Jesus pointed out; she proved it could be done. And Jesus invites you to follow the same path: "Whoever is a little one, let him come to me."

Now go to sleep.

SAINT JOHN NEUMANN
An American Saint

Part One

Most of the time, when we talk about saints, we are dealing with holy people who went home to God a long time ago, but in this story of Bishop John Neumann (new-man) we are talking about one who became a saint not too many years ago. That is, he was *declared* a saint a few years ago: to become a saint takes a lifetime.

All parents must shiver a bit when the next child in line begins to ask why? why? why? As a young boy John had this very bad. In fact, he wanted the whole world explained to him. A cat or a dog takes what comes and reacts angrily or indifferently or quietly or happily, while the beautiful spirit that is a human child takes nothing for granted and questions every step along the way. No wonder God loves this young soul. Like him, it can know. And love follows knowledge, if what we know is beautiful like God and his Son Jesus.

In the case of little John, he had an unhappy habit of waking the family at three o'clock in the morning to let them know that the moon and the earth had not dropped out of sight yet, and please, tell me once more what keeps them up?

Bright Young Boy

Now God made John Neumann pretty smart. For instance, he could speak many languages by the time he left the priests' seminary school. And he was an outstanding pupil in all his studies while getting ready to become a priest. However, those who write about him insist that he worked and worked and worked to gather whatever might help him in his work for Jesus. For instance, he learned to speak French by going to a seminary where only French was spoken. He learned English by hanging around a factory where the workers spoke English. He learned Italian by setting aside each day a special time for studying it.

Maybe you are a young person who likes to study about flowers and leaves. You would get along fine with Johnny because he liked these things so much that his beautiful collection of them is still in a museum in Munich. Did you know that the study of flowers and leaves has brought people to believe in God? Yes, that is true, especially in the case of a certain man who was a great leader in the study of insects. He was finally brought to God and to God's Church and was a very holy person. One day someone asked him, "What made you become a Christian?" The great professor looked at him, smiled, and answered, "Bugs." And those who studied how bugs are put together knew what he meant.

Even while quite young, John had a feeling that he must stay very close to God. He decided that he wanted to be a priest. Each day he prayed God for the help he needed, as he prepared himself to bring Jesus to his people. He asked especially for the patience and the courage necessary for the vocation he had chosen.

If we follow John along as he prepares to become a priest, we find a very, very sad young man. The bishop of his diocese told him that there was no need for any new priests there. This meant that John's ordination would be put off for a good while. But Neumann was not one to run to a corner and cry out his heart. He understood that a great cross and great suffering can return us to God as usable, willing servants.

Our young hero knew that suffering would make him a follower on the road to Calvary. He really joined hands and voice with Jesus when he cried in his great suffering in the garden, "Father, not my will but thy will be done." And, as it came out, the actual facts would turn him very much into a young follower of Christ. It became clear that if he wanted to be a priest he would have to leave everything — his mother and father, his family, his home, his very country — for the sweet sake of the suffering Jesus.

America Calls

Although John had a difficult time with the bishops of Europe, there is no doubt that fame and honor would have been his at home, due to his great talents. America meant hiddenness for him, sort of the minor leagues, as far as Europe was concerned. But he decided to go there nevertheless. Then came the day for leaving home. Bohemians are warm of heart, and John knew his own heart. When the morning came for him to leave, he quietly ate breakfast before his family woke up. Too many hearts would be broken at too many tender good-byes. He had found himself upon two occasions falling into a chair and trembling all over at the thought of his departure. Quietly he left his home, alone in the dawn.

There followed months upon months of waiting. The government refused to give him a passport, and the bishops would not give him permission to leave Bohemia. His money was about gone and he had to borrow from priest to priest.

(Remember that Neumann was not even ordained yet, because he simply had not been accepted by any bishop in Europe or in America. And this was necessary before he could be ordained.)

Finally, he got the proper permissions, and he was ready to bid farewell to Europe. But how did the American future look? Two dioceses would not accept him and his life offering. Even the officials in Philadelphia, whose future bishop he would become and in whose service he would die, wrote that they did not need him. Like the Infant Jesus, there was no room in the inn; and like the man Jesus, he came into his own and his own received him not.

However, nothing stopped John Neumann. As they say, "When the going gets tough, the tough get going." John made a last appeal and the Bishop of New York, John DuBois, accepted him. At last John Neumann, sick to his heart with loneliness, walked aboard his ship. The year was 1836.

(He would come home again nineteen years later, come home as the bishop of Philadelphia, then one of the greatest dioceses in the New World.)

His New Life

So we turn now to John Neumann's new life. After his arrival in New York he began his final studies for ordination to the priesthood. But the bishop gave him another moment of special happiness at this time. As he prepared himself to become a priest, he prepared the little children in the cathedral parish for their first Holy Communion.

Once John Neumann became Father John Neumann, he left for his first appointment in the far-flung diocese of New York. There was a German-speaking settlement of Catholics in the northwest corner of the state — right near Niagara Falls — and

the bishop asked John to go out to these people. The name of the place was Williamsville, and the church had no floor or roof or steeple. The parish measured 900 square miles, and Williamsville had the largest Catholic church in the area.

A sick call today means that the priest gets in his automobile and rolls out to wherever the sick person is. To John, out in Williamsville, a sick call meant a day's journey. It usually included walking at least half the way — often with frozen feet and, at times, with a fever John was subject to. There were Indians, too, but these Indians loved the blackrobes, as they called the priests, and again and again they would find him and tenderly carry him home. The Indians knew that he was sicker than the patient. At this point in his life must have come the famous moment of his riding a horse backward. You see, our John was not used to riding. Putting the wrong foot in the stirrup first, he found himself looking where he had been instead of where he was going. Anyway, everybody who saw him on a horse knew that he had no business there, and the horse knew it too. It is a picture best passed over with love.

John had all kinds of different people within his parish. There were the French people, the Irish, and lots of rosy-cheeked

Germans. They were all finding their way to this other "Christ" who had no doubt cried out with his Master, "And I — once I am lifted up from earth — will draw all men to myself."

Meanwhile, the list of work to be done grew and grew. He must build a schoolhouse, and therein he would teach four hours a day. He must take care of the sick, so he studied medicine. He ate — whatever they gave him. Once a week, the smoke came from his chimney and that meant he was having his one hot meal. The good people wanted to help, but he said that bread and butter and cheese would do quite well.

Decision to Become a Redemptorist

It was during these years that John met a Redemptorist missionary whose name was Father Prost. Having heard this man preach a parish mission, he was much impressed by the Redemptorist way of life. The idea of preaching in one parish after another a series of sermons on the basic truths of life — that some day we will die, be judged, and receive reward or punishment according to the way we have lived — appealed to him immensely. He began to think seriously of joining the Redemptorist Congregation.

Now the greatest secret of John Neumann was that he had sworn to follow Jesus. And this he had done; he lived in a frozen Niagara hut, often without food, always without ordinary comforts. But he wanted to bind himself even more closely to Jesus the Redeemer by taking the vows of religion called poverty, chastity, and obedience. Already at his ordination he had promised obedience to his bishop. When he became a priest he accepted the fact that he was to remain unmarried. And his life since his ordination had been living proof that he was truly poor as Jesus was poor. He gave up everything to be closer to our Lord who had nothing. Money to him was an extra suitcase he did not need to lug along to heaven. He believed that the things of this world are all so many rungs on the ladder, and that if he hung on the bottom rungs (whether they were wealth or pleasure or power), he would never reach the top of the ladder.

Why then did he wish to become a Redemptorist? Simply because he wanted to join a community of men whose prayer life at home would so increase their personal love of God that it would overflow into the hearts of the people to whom they preached on the missions. He wanted to be part of a team of men who prayed over and preached about the good news of God's love for all people.

Certainly, this man already had the missionary heart to console the sick and to offer Christ's mercy and ransom in the confessional. And so the Redemptorists gathered him in. John now began his novitiate — a period of time during which he was to absorb the Redemptorist spirit in preparation for his taking the three vows. Because of the shortage of priests at that time, he did not remain in one place as a novice; while preparing himself with prayer he was sent from one Redemptorist parish to another to help where he was most needed. The novice rule calls for humility, simplicity, and zeal; but these were already his life signs and his way of life.

Now go to sleep. We'll continue this story of our saint at another time.

Part Two

(We left John Neumann preparing to take his vows as a Redemptorist. Born in Bohemia, he began studying for the priesthood in his native land. But because there were more than enough priests in his homeland his ordination was delayed. He applied to the bishops in the New World and was accepted by the Bishop of New York. Ordained there, he worked long and hard in the northwest part of the state. Then, since he admired the Redemptorists so much, he decided to become one of them.)

John Neumann made his vows as a Redemptorist on January 16, 1842, at St. James Church in Baltimore, Maryland. He immediately became a member of the Redemptorist mission band, bringing God's word to Maryland, Virginia, Pennsylvania, and Ohio. It was a hard life, but very satisfying, because now he preached to thousands he could not reach before.

In due time, John Neumann was appointed pastor of one of the Redemptorist parishes in the Northeast. Those who lived with him at this time — and later in other parishes — marveled at his untiring zeal. He took all the night sick calls, and that meant he must hurry out to wherever the runner directed him. Then he would come home, make a wood fire for the others, and retire to the house chapel for the five o'clock morning meditation.

This was John's life beat — to work unheralded in the dark for others. There, hidden with Christ, we find a saint plying his trade of love for God and love of neighbor.

When we are unkind to nature, nature will demand payment in full. At this time there was a very mournful list of John's health problems — diseased lungs, broken constitution, and a persistent grinding cough. Death seemed about to demand its full payment, but John's life was still ahead of him in the mind of the almighty Creator.

Did he fear death? No. He looked it in the eye. He knew that it could come at any time, and he never forgot it for a waking moment. He had long ago slammed the door on earthly pleasures, and when the gates of heaven were ready to swing out for him he would be ready for them.

Chosen to Lead American Redemptorists

Some years later, the unbelievable happened: John was chosen as leader of all the American Redemptorists. When he heard the rumor, he laughed in disbelief. He was a man who honestly believed that he should remain in the ranks. On the other hand, the cold facts were that if they put him into a spot where hard work was the order of the day, they had picked the right man. Needless to say, John, in his humility, did not even write his parents about his new position in the Redemptorist Congregation.

When he arrived in New York City to take over his new job, he was so humbly dressed that the associate lay Brother who answered the door of the rectory did not recognize him. But once established there he went to work with vigor and vitality. Working side by side with the Notre Dame Sisters, he set out to improve the Catholic education of the children in all Redemptorist parishes. And he had the courage to hold the line when others wanted to overexpand in the Redemptorist parishes located in New York, Maryland, and Pennsylvania.

Now, despite all this activity, there were some who disliked him. He was young and had been a Redemptorist only five years, and there were those who did not want him in charge. Perhaps their intentions were good, but they formed a group to get him out. Neumann couldn't ignore all this; he was very sensitive. Friends advised him to resign, so he wrote to Rome, asking to be removed from the office. His resignation was accepted, and another Redemptorist took his place. He did all this not because he resented criticism but because he was afraid that the unhappy minority would shake the portals of the Congregation. Now, back in the ranks, he was a very happy Redemptorist priest.

He Becomes a Bishop

But his happiness would not be for long. He did not know it, but a new cross, a new honor, was casting its shadow over him. An associate lay Brother said that he had seen Father Neumann in a vision, and he was wearing the garments of a bishop. Neumann suggested that the Brother see a doctor. Even his friends laughed, saying that Neumann wanted to be a bishop as much as a bear wants a trap.

But the shadow was coming closer. At this time he was stationed in Baltimore, and Archbishop Kenrick used to make his confession to John Neumann each week. On one occasion when the confession was over, the archbishop sat across from Neumann and sized him up, "Yes, you can do it. You will look fine in a bishop's outfit," he said half playfully. Hoping that the archbishop had not been serious, Neumann wrote to his Redemptorist superiors and Kenrick himself, telling them that to make him a bishop was unthinkable. He begged the nuns to pray especially for him.

However, Kenrick had not been fooling. He walked into the Redemptorist rectory one dusk, sought out Neumann's room, and left a bishop's ring and cross on the desk of the absent Neumann. Well, no one fights Rome, really. A man's faith has to be as strong as his humility; he can only cry with the Master, "Father, not my will but thy will be done." So, on Passion Sunday in the year 1852, John Neumann accepted the will of God. He had this to say: "If our Lord gave me the choice, either to die or to accept the episcopate, I would lay down my life tomorrow." And Neumann meant what he said.

Like Alphonsus, the founder of the Redemptorist Congregation, Neumann had made a vow never to lose a minute of time. He kept his promise by making every work a prayer. And he had plenty of work to do in his new assignment. As Bishop of Philadelphia, he had 35,000 square miles to take care of, a million people, a hundred priests.

He was no holy-card saint. On the very day after his first Sunday Mass in his Cathedral Church, two murderers gained headlines, and they were appointed to die the next day. No one had been able to get them to make their peace with God. But the new bishop went to them, prayed with them, and helped them at last to make good confessions. (Two good thieves instead of one?)

His Work in Philadelphia

Being a bishop, of course, is not easy. John Neumann was forever mending fences, as it were. There were always problems to be solved, complaints to be answered.

One of the difficulties he had to face was opposition to the Catholic faith and to the education of Catholic children. Remember, this was almost 150 years ago, and some people who were not Catholic resented those who were Catholic. They felt that a person who had to obey the pope — who lived in Rome — could not be a true American. And, because of this mistaken patriotism, they would burn down Catholic buildings. (You should thank God that you are free now to attend the church and school of your choice.)

John Neumann had shown his intense interest in Catholic schools when he headed the Redemptorists. As leader of the diocese of Philadelphia, he continued his efforts in this area. When he came there, the city had two parochial schools; at his death eight years later, there were 100 of them. Besides this, he rebuilt many old churches or founded new ones during his time in office.

As a bishop, John Neumann was no longer bound by the Redemptorist rule, but he was still a Redemptorist at heart.

Morning, noon, and night, he acted as missionary to his people. No other priest at the cathedral heard more confessions than he did. One advantage here was that he could speak so many languages. The New World attracted many people from Europe in those days, and Catholics who sought the comforts of religion were happy to find a priest — and a bishop at that — who could understand them and speak to them in their native tongue.

Why He Is Remembered

When John Neumann first came to Philadelphia, he could not speak Gaelic. Tearfully, he told the Irish people that he could not speak their language. But what did he do? He began to study it, and before long knew it quite well. As proof, the story is told about a little old Irish lady who confessed to him in Gaelic and came out of the confessional crying, "Thank God, we have an Irish bishop at last." Truly, John Neumann was "all things to all people," as St. Paul wanted us all to be.

Quite often the bishop would preach retreats to his own priests, bringing them together for talks on the spiritual side of their lives. It was no wonder that other dioceses wanted him to lead their retreats, since his own priests would pass along the good word.

Often he would visit his own seminary and teach these future priests about life out on the missions. And wherever he went, he impressed on his listeners the importance of the morning offering: Whatever I do today, I do for you, my Jesus.

Saint John Neumann will ever have a place of honor for bringing the love of the Eucharistic Christ to the lives of millions of people. He introduced into the United States what we call the Forty Hours Devotion. (Please explain, Mom or Dad.)

His Last Days

We can see from the life of John Neumann that saints are not born saints. They are made — by the grace of God and by their own willingness to live God's life fully within them. They worked hard so that the People of God could see the Spirit working within them. They believed that they would have plenty of time to rest for all eternity.

John Neumann did get back to his beloved home in Bohemia. And the church bells rang out to honor the returning son. Then once more he held his father in his arms; and together they visited his mother's grave. John did not know it then, but this would be the last meeting with his father here on earth.

As he prepared to leave for America, a neighborhood friend took him aside and talked to him in deep, tragic tones, "John, you are going on a long and dangerous voyage. Now, take my advice." His two callused fingers dug into a worn purse and carefully drew forth two gold coins. And, lowering his voice significantly, he said, "Now, when you board the ship, slip these coins into the captain's hand and say, 'Captain, here are two pieces of gold on condition that you always steer the ship in the shallow water near the shore.' " And then came the triumphant climax, "Should anything happen to the ship, in this way you could save yourself by swimming."

That is the story that Neumann told the day he died. Whatever else he did, it was never in his makeup to stay near the shore. He set his compass straight for the New World and conquered it. There would be no port but Philadelphia — no port but sainthood.

John Neumann died in Philadelphia on January 5, 1860. He was declared a saint by God's Church on June 19, 1977.

Now go to sleep.